Your Personal SuperComputer

Robert Young

From The Author

This book was inspired by the general observation of what people demonstrate to one another every day.

It has been prepared as a gift to every person on earth in reflection of the great abilities and resources available to humanity.

With respect and honor I now invite you personally, to enjoy the revelation and jump into that world of magic and miracles that you have demonstrated since childhood.

Love and Harmony,

Robert

www.youngsight.com

Chapter 1

Our Personal Supercomputer is an integral part of our being that manages the many mysteries of life and the incredible events that often occur out of nowhere. With the advancement of humanity, we are now ready to introduce the extended capabilities of our personal supercomputer and highlight its practical advantages in our everyday life.

In each person we have known from the beginning about the presence of "something special" and have all marveled at the sometimes superhuman, feats performed by people in emergency or highly emotional circumstances. This "something special" has been the subject of many studies and disciplines have been developed in an attempt to tap into the magic of this superhuman capability. We are now ready to open the door and reveal the simplicity that has been hidden in front of everyone and bring to life the capabilities that have been confused by complexity for many thousands of years.

The synchronicities that have led us from one situation in life to another have often taken our breath with joy and amazement when we look back to how it could not have been planned by the most advanced of computers.

These events are controlled by our individual supercomputers and can be initialized by simply knowing that it is possible. Without explanation, we proceed to work miracles and have no idea how this happens but it certainly happens and can continue to happen if we consciously agree to have this as part of our life.

At some time in our life many of us can relate to the "accident that should have happened" but, because of some unexplainable shift in events, the accident was evaded and our personal safety was maintained. Our personal supercomputer is connected to the interface between our being and the physical world and is capable of warping reality to bring to us the result we desire at any moment.

Our uncanny ability to know what is happening to a loved-one, even at a distance, is something that suddenly appears without introduction and has no link to any event that we are aware of at the time. Our personal supercomputer monitors everything about us and will signal us when it feels the necessity. It opens us to the unknown and allows us to experience those things that seem to come out of nowhere.

Many other unexplained human phenomena, lead us to a missing link that gives rise to the possibility that we are more than meets the eye, and certainly more than we, as intelligent beings, have ever considered possible.

At the moment, it may seem like "our personal supercomputer" is a concept that is used to explain the workings of the human anatomy. In reality, our personal supercomputer really exists, and is available for our extended use, should we wish to take advantage of such an advanced and unusual capability in our life.

In order to take advantage of your Personal Super Computer (PSC), you must first see how it works in your everyday life, so that you may extend its capabilities and leave behind the complications and complexities that have been developed through centuries of research and experimentation. This means that you must throw away everything you know and start again from a point of total simplicity. What will be revealed is what already exists deep inside your being, and the familiarity will prove that there is nothing to learn even though there is much to be revealed.

Chapter 2

The Story begins with the screech of a young child running playfully with total abandon from the hands of a loving relative. The rush of excitement fills the air and suddenly there is a frightening "crunch" as the little one runs headlong into a roughcast brick wall. Silence engulfs the scene as everyone watches the small body fold into oblivion against the bricks, then suddenly bounce off and fall heavily onto the cement floor.

The emotions of the onlookers are triggered and the natural sense of protection for the young child bursts to the surface in a gasp, almost rendering their body useless. Reflexes suddenly fly into action but before anyone can reach the child a familiar screech of excitement emanates from the bundle on the floor and a beaming face looks up and laughs as if the collision was the best part of the game. At this point, the mother laughs with the child and quickly dissipates the force of concern coming from the relatives while the picture of amazement fills the eyes of everyone present.

In one form or another, this scene is part of everyone's life and it is well known that a child can survive many things if the influence of our experience is not imposed on the child.

In the scene above, there would have been major consequences if the influences of the onlookers had reached the child. There would be cuts and bruises and possibly a long stay in hospital to repair the damage caused by the bricks, but as it stands, the child has revealed the enormous capability of his or her personal supercomputer and allowed it to work without consideration or interpretation.

The child's capability is clear but if it is said that you have the same capability, you would simply answer "I am not a child". The enormity of the division of each person from their personal supercomputer is quickly revealed, and further amplified by many simple statements that we use in our life to continue the separation. Our logic makes sure that we can never consciously access our personal supercomputer.

The greatest function in our logic that can bring about change is 'proof', and the greatest tool we use to overshadow 'proof' is verbal programming or analysis. We convince ourselves, every few minutes, that we cannot do things and that nothing can be done without knowing 'how'.

Even when the proof is in front of us, we tend to isolate ourselves and say "I don't know how to do that". The fact is, you came into the world with a personal supercomputer and no one can take that away from you. It is also true, that as a child you had no idea of how it worked, so why should you attempt to know before you actually use this magnificent capability of your personal supercomputer.

Because of the many centuries of education and experience in the logical physical world, it is now necessary for many human formalities to be dispelled to allow firstly, the presence of the unknown and secondly, the practical use of the unknown in the same way that the uninfluenced young child unknowingly demonstrates with great perfection, the use of his or her personal supercomputer.

On another level it is important to note the influence of the mother in consolidating the process and welcoming the miracle of instantaneous healing into the physical world. The obvious elation of the child was accepted and amplified by the mother, which allowed the process to be completed and solidified as part of the child's reality.

With every application of our personal super computer there is a function that cannot be ignored and will appear each time. The final welcoming of the outcome into the physical world is always carried out by a second person. This part of the process is simple, but sometimes not obvious to the person or persons involved in the processes of the personal supercomputer.

The secret is in the involvement of a like-minded person who is willing to accept whatever you deliver to the world. Where there are no witnesses the miracle appears and is accepted in the physical world, but in practice, there will be interaction with interested parties at some stage, and consolidation will depend on the majority of these parties accepting the possibility of the impossible, and welcoming it at a moments notice. The joy of being able to express what has happened in your life, will consolidate the miracle, and make room for more magic to appear in your life.

Chapter 3

As the story continues, the scene changes to a car travelling through the night, the lights of oncoming cars distort and dance through the drizzling rain. Signs appear as sudden flashes with half read distorted messages blocked out by reflections from a passing car. The delayed message, 'one lane bridge' floats around looking for clarity, when out of nowhere, the sudden blast of four high powered headlights reaches deep into your reality and the massive blast of a truck horn informs you clearly that you are about to have a 'head on' collision with the biggest truck you have ever seen in your life. There is no room on the bridge and nowhere to go. Your heart almost stops as you brace for the impact, then all of a sudden the lights are gone, there is no rain and all you are aware of is total silence. The truck has gone and you are on the other side of the bridge. Are you still alive? What has happened?

It takes some time to settle and as you realize you are still driving, the first question is answered. You are alive, still driving somewhere, but with no sense of direction. As you stop the car you feel the elation of still being alive, and your eyes close for a moment of contemplation.

In a matter of moments the noise of the traffic returns, your eyes open, and to your amazement you can see the lights and the rain are as they were before the truck appeared. You confirm that the bridge is behind you and as you open the car door, you can hear the truck horn disappearing into the distance.

Something abnormally wonderful has happened to maintain your safety; reality has somehow been distorted and placed you on the other side of the bridge. You drive on knowing that you are totally safe. Your life has been changed, and you wonder how you will ever convince another person of the solid reality of what just happened.

It can be said that it was 'not your time', or that 'someone is looking after you', and these things can very well be true. The fact that this actually happened, indicates what is possible when a person's deepest desire interfaces with the physical world and changes what is considered to be an inevitable reality.

Your personal supercomputer has acted in a way that you could not imagine, and it is easy to hide this fact by using historical teachings and opinions to analyse it into oblivion.

The fact remains, that your personal supercomputer has abilities that can affect the outcome of events in the physical world, and can change what would be accepted as normal in our present experience.

There are simple observations that occur regularly in our lives, which offset all arguments and allow us to attribute these events, and all the special feelings, to our personal supercomputer. The most effective example is the process of walking on hot coals, and not experiencing the first-degree burns that are usually inflicted when the powers of your personal supercomputer are denied. The simple knowledge that you will not be burned, is all that is needed to allow your personal supercomputer to come into action.

This is one of the most complex and controversial applications of our personal supercomputer, which for many, brings forth emotions and reactions from "totally amazing" to "frightening and creepy". No matter what our reaction may be, the ultimate outcome is the intervention in events in a totally miraculous manner, to change our interface with the world and maintain our security in times of impending disaster.

Chapter 4

IF we now take ourselves to the bustling streets of Manhattan where a couple from Australia have just had their first experience of the rush from Wall Street station to the streets surrounding the extinct World Trade Centre, you will feel the shock, as the couple realize that their only mode of communication has suddenly failed. The faithful iPhone with all its maps and telephone numbers has suddenly decided to stop working.

Their appointment with a close relative, who works in one of the surrounding multi story buildings, was critical to their planned trip to the city and unless they met John on that day they would not be able to link up with him before their return to Australia.

The situation seemed hopeless; neither of them could remember the phone number or the name of the company where John works.

Without reason, Mary looked up and saw a man sitting at a table in front of a small restaurant. She was immediately attracted to him and without question, walked over, excused herself, and asked, "Do you work around here".

The immediate answer of "Yes" started a sequence of events that Mary and Bill still talk about today.

When Mary asked her new found friend Clint for assistance in recollecting the name of the company where John worked his reply was,
"I work at the office of Swanton Distributors".
Mary almost fell over. She recognized the name immediately.
"That is where John works. We were to ring him when we arrived but our phone decided to stop working."
"Are you John's Aunt Mary? He was expecting you a bit later. I came down to have an early lunch so he would be free to lunch with you. Sit down and I will give him a ring."
Of all the possible combinations you can imagine, Mary picked the very person who was part of her overall plan. The unknown link from her personal supercomputer was provided from another plane to continue the flow and complete a story that could never have been imagined at the time.

This synchronicity is one of many that occur every day which makes it possible for our individual experiences to exist in a complex world.

For thousands of years, these synchronicities have been experienced and many methods have been developed in an attempt to control this phenomenon. All the developed methods have given the process credibility but in general, this natural phenomenon is known as something that 'just happens'. All the disciplined processes of the past are no longer necessary, or even considered. Education and experience do not determine the eligibility of a person to receive messages, and the circumstances do not depend on whether you know about such things or not. In fact, the more unaware you are the more likely you are to experience a miracle.

It seems like there must be a conclusion that can be drawn from what we have observed. However, the development of a 'conclusion' of any sort will achieve what it says. The process of synchronicity will be concluded or stopped, and there will be no more opportunity until your 'conclusion' is dispelled. It is like driving a car at high speed, all you do is observe and enjoy the demonstration of your skills without any analysis of what is required.

Chapter 5

The streets were relatively clear as the small groups of surfers started their walk from the bus stop towards the local beach. The warmth of the sun and the slight characteristic scent of the coastal breeze seemed to take everyone to another dimension where the dream of a perfect wave took the place of the task at hand.

The natural rhythm of the walk took on its own character, but the sudden echo of a dull thud reverberating through the air, followed by an uncharacteristic expletive, rocked the silence and captured the attention of everyone in the street. Jimmy had walked straight into a light pole and crashed to the ground with his board bag stretched across his head in the most unlikely position.

The street rocked with laughter and lighthearted ridicule. Jimmy became the star of the day. He had left behind the mechanism that allowed him to walk around safely in the world. His awareness went to another dimension without first making sure he was safe. His personal supercomputer was diverted to the generation and testing of a reality that he expected to come his way once he reached the water. He was 'day dreaming'.

The shock of the sudden collision echoed throughout his body and his awareness became intense as he passed the next light pole. He shrunk a little as he heard the cheer from the crowd for successfully navigating the pole. The reprogramming by observation had started, by the third pole the cheering had stopped and the light poles had disappeared out of his field once again. The unknown sense that detects light poles quickly fell into place and released his vision to capture other things that were much more attractive to a young boy.

There are many things that we experience on a daily basis that prove beyond a doubt that there is much more happening in our field than we realize. We have senses and abilities that serve us in many ways, and continue to do so as long as our awareness is switched to the timeline that we intend to reside in. Much of what we do in everyday life is supported by functions that we never need to access. Our personal supercomputer is on standby all the time and will provide what is necessary as long as we allow it to work.

We are free to work whichever way we wish, but at the slightest intention of our 'taking over', our personal supercomputer gives up its connection to the physical world and reverts to the position of neutral, acting like power steering in a car; giving assistance but not taking on the steering.

The level to which you encourage the use of your personal supercomputer is up to you but failing to encourage its use is like walking a horse that is ready to ride. You may think it is good to be cautious, but it is much better to climb on the horse and experience the majesty of the ride.

This unusual introduction of one of the most extensive applications of our personal supercomputer opens the way to much discussion, and many examples of unknown senses that appear in our body can be contributed to a process instigated by our personal supercomputer. Unlike the detection sense, that tells your system where the light poles are, these other unknown senses instigate physical changes either in or outside the body to affect unspecified physical outputs that adjust your interface to the world and make a major difference in your life.

Every day, more senses are exposed and our connection to the events of the world becomes more harmonious.

The old habit that developed over the centuries, calls on all these unspecified senses or feelings to be captured and called 'emotion'. All 'so called' emotions cause immediate reaction when the body is asked to respond to something that is blocked in a definition.

The unspecified feeling called 'emotion' has no connection to your personal supercomputer and therefore remains in the body as reaction. In the past this unfortunate habit has led to a life of emotional reaction rather than a life of magic and miracles. The allowance of undefined and unknown senses and outputs, from the body and all its surrounds, will make room for the magic and miracles that emanate from the induced harmony of your personal supercomputer.

Chapter 6

The silhouette of Paul's small frame against the morning sun would have gone unnoticed were it not for the expressive glow of his face as he watched every move of his father's hands as they skillfully assembled the final parts of his bike, ready for his birthday, the next morning.

The sparkle of the new spokes captured his gaze as he recollected the magic of how a tiny bundle of spokes grew into a brilliantly spinning wheel. Paul had been given the honor of watching his promised, seven year old birthday present, come to life from a rusty old frame found in his uncle's garage. It had taken many weeks, but now the beautifully painted and transferred frame was accepting its working parts, ready for tomorrow's celebration.

Paul was ready in every way. He had made his own preparation and had arranged his own lessons to graduate to a "big bike". His Uncle Frank had agreed to teach Paul as best he could on a bike that was too big for a seven year old and much to his surprise found himself standing in amazement as Paul took over after three attempts.

He rode off down the footpath, catching each pedal at the top of its stroke, pushing as far as his legs would allow, until finally his steering let him down. A very frightening moment passed, and he found himself holding on to the top of a fence, with his legs awkwardly wrapped around the bike frame to prevent it falling.

Over the past few weeks, there had been a strange sense of cooperation in every part of this project and everyone seemed to know exactly what would suit Paul. Everything either thrilled him immensely or met with surprising acceptance and approval. There were some items that he found to be out of place but somehow he knew everything was working to plan. The brakes looked old and the seat and handle grips did not fit his picture but he was only six and had no real say in these matters. Things may be different when he is seven. Little did Paul know that tomorrow's presents from his relatives included a new set of racing style brakes, a junior racing seat and a set of cross country handle bar grips, just like he imagined.

Paul's dream had been welcomed into the world and although it was controlled by his personal supercomputer, it had produced a series of incentives and circumstances that lifted the world of everyone involved. This allowed his project to fill their lives with the desire they felt to fulfill their part of the dream.

Paul had no idea of how to produce a bike from the practical world, but he did know how to produce a bike out of nowhere. The expressive glow of his face showed his immense satisfaction, at watching his heart's desire appear as a reality, without any direction from him at all.

There is something to note that at first may seem rather abstract, but there is a hidden and unique quality about a child which makes sure you know their likes and dislikes without any need for thought. It is not difficult to satisfy their desires when they are not directly involved, and at times of special celebration, everything seems to work without a hitch. This is because it remains under the control of the child's supercomputer and the desires of an adult are not substituted for those of a child.

In general, it is your desire to satisfy what you feel about a child and in this way you are working in harmony with the child's personal supercomputer.

It is not the same if you attempt to meet the child's desires while bypassing your own personal supercomputer. Your divine connection may be misinterpreted and you can find yourself out of tune with their hidden heart's desires.

The children of today are able to present to the world much more than we can imagine, and the struggle that comes from the unknown uniqueness of the child appears only when we fail to make space for it in the physical world.

In a fraction of a second, a child can beam to you a brilliant picture of who they are and then continue to play as if nothing happened.

It is our purpose to accept their picture and the breathtaking burst of light that carries it and accept it into the world in all its glory without change or comment. This builds a multi-dimensional space in the world that belongs to that child, where it can live and work its magic throughout the remainder of its life.

A passing glance from a child, you may never see again, can be your opportunity to welcome that child into the world and recognize the full extent of the divinity where their personal supercomputer resides and awaits its opportunity to work with the harmony of the child's hidden heart's desires.

Chapter 7

The examples and stories can go on forever, but the greatest thing in everyone's life is when the supercomputer jumps into action and exceeds our personal expectations in ways that we could never imagine.

We can all relate to the special events shown on television where, in a singing competition, the most unlikely person begins to sing a song that most people would not attempt and completely "blows away" the preconception of the judges and the audience to leave them shocked, ecstatic and emotional all at the same time. The feeling is unbelievable and without a doubt, from another place that we only know as majestic.

The spirit of every person has been aroused and the superhuman part of everyone shows a recognition that brings in something alive and presents everyone in a much higher place than they were in moments before. The special gift that came through one person aroused everyone's spirit and each time the event is replayed, it performs the same magic to a person listening for the first time, as it did when it first occurred.

Within this event, there is a gift that everyone would love to capture and be able to repeat at will. Every attempt to do this has finally dwindled away and failed because we failed to see what actually happened.

Once the spirit is aroused to the extent where it makes you leap out of your chair, there is nothing you can do to stop it. There is no sense of consideration and even a broken leg will not stop you leaping out of your chair.

It is not the song or the singer or the home run that excites your spirit. It is a sequence of events that reveal a sudden recognition of brilliance from your origin, and allows you to switch into unlimited mode, surpassing the normal level of your scope and appreciation of everything in the physical world. The floodgates are opened and all your emotion and appreciation pours out for everyone to see.

If it were possible to allow these ecstatic moments to fill your life, it would not be possible to continue without burning ourselves out or gradually pushing such things into the background and looking for something else to excite our lives.

With the present visual structure of our lives and our physical body, we have no provision for the continued action of exciting our spirit and surpassing all limitations. Just as we have no way of controlling how reality is distorted to protect our wellbeing. A slight change in our visual structure and a reformatting of our value reference, will allow for continuous access to the reality that can not only produce the unimaginable, but can support it in the physical world.

The reality of your personal supercomputer can be seen by everyone, and all you need to do is allow it to exist so that it can be recognized and accepted by the part of your being that allows its operation.

You are much more than the physical being that you imagine; even if you are fully advanced and educated in everything that we can possible know on earth. No matter how far you go, you will never solve the mysteries of the physical being, let alone the mysteries of the divine human being that you are. With this in mind, we must find a way to access our personal supercomputer and have it provide all the things that we believe it can provide.

There is no simple answer even though the best answer that can be provided is contained in one word, "simplicity". In every event, where the personal supercomputer seems to jump into life, there is a sense of simplicity. In an unbelievable complex set of circumstances everything was aligned to provide a simple but miraculous outcome. To use what we are looking at, we must look to the simplicity and innocence of a child and all that is present to hold that simplicity and allow the advent of a miraculous event.

If you look closely at a child's movement, you will see that each movement follows something that is outside our visual range. It is like something moves first and the child happily follows in complete oblivion of everything around them. You will even see a sudden change of pattern when the child notices an adult watching. It is as if they have been caught doing something wrong, their pace slows and they move with a sense of caution until they feel they are free from the expected adult influence.

Left to its own resources a child will move to the dance of its spirit with great freedom and total abandon of all external considerations.

In doing so, there is a sparkle in their eye and an ability to absorb whatever they need for the thrill of the adventure they feel in that moment. The transmission of mischief is clear and their eyes grow bigger as they absorb the vision of their next intention. A crawling infant can outmaneuver a parent in a moment and arrive at an open cupboard before there is even a thought of what is happening.

It is obvious that a child's operating system is much different to an adult or a teenager and our consideration that the child has a lot to learn almost totally negates our ability to see the great advantages of a totally unencumbered spirit directly connected to our unique physical motivation system. The possibility of a motivation system that is totally segregated from our highly programmed logical mind would excite the greatest of scientists and here it is looking us in the face every day of our lives. The love and excitement surrounding a child who is not yet at the point of taking on logic is something to experience, and the times throughout life, when this same condition shows itself, become treasures that we never forget.

Chapter 8

Our personal supercomputer cannot be tracked in a linear manner or depicted from any one angle and it is not definable in our language even though we can understand it in a moment. It is not controllable in any way, even though it provides all our needs and is ready to provide more at a moment's notice.

To assist in our understanding, we must once again look at the attributes and actions of a child to see more clearly what we aspired to when we landed on this earthly plane.

Almost every child in the world knows what to do when they are dressed as a fairy and given a magic wand. Male or female makes no difference to the response. There is a sudden twinkle in their eyes and a rush to spread their magic to everyone who needs it. Tinkerbelle sparkles are considered natural and the sparkle that emanates from each child lights up something intangible in the lives of everyone involved.

All the theory we have about the way we are "made up" or how we are connected to our origin has no place in the life of a child but the magic and joy of what we class as fiction, seems to take first place every time.

If you ask a small child to say some prayers to God they will immediately look up at a specific angle where their total attention switches to the divine and they will proceed to communicate, without a moment's hesitation, to a realm that is obviously outside the physical vision of the average adult. There is a specific position and visual attention that connects us to the divine or unseen world that interfaces with our personal supercomputer and encourages the delivery of gifts that we would never imagine to be available.

The process of prayer has been encouraged over the centuries and has been used successfully on many occasions but if you look at the child you will find that you can take away the seriousness and the focus of religion and be in continuous contact without knowing or caring about "how".

It is not unusual to see a child suddenly stop in a trance-like state watching someone or listening to something that is not available to us. It also far from unusual to find that one of your children is entertaining an invisible childhood friend and demanding that he or she is accepted as part of your family.

These superhuman capabilities that these children are demonstrating have been lost to society but with a reawakening of the immense value of these gifts to society each person's personal supercomputer will jump back into the action and redevelop the interface needed to connect the unknown back into our lives.

The thrill of being able to communicate what you see, feel or hear to another person without any feeling of criticism or opinion has disappeared from the world and the consideration of listening to the visionary pictures of someone looking into another world has been taken away from everyday life and placed in the hands of the so called "professionals" to turn it into a business. Our children, however, know nothing of our rules and many times know well before time what is happening and what must be attracted or avoided.

Our personal supercomputer remains on standby at all times and will produce whatever is necessary to support the joy of existence by means of magic and miracles that emanate from the unknown and appear in the physical world to smooth our path.

Chapter 9

Now that we are aware of the presence of our personal supercomputer, it is a good time to look further at some of the practical examples of how to apply our special gift and feel the results of the intervention of our personal supercomputer.

The story continues with a group of Scouts walking through the vast outskirts of the beautiful "Blue Mountains". The four-day trek had been difficult and James could see the end coming near as he took a mark on the nearby hills to determine their location. Everything seemed to be in order and they were on track to be able to see civilization before the day was out. The 'off track' shortcut had proven to be a good move and the next track should be appearing soon. The map was a little short on detail but it was confirmed by the GPS that the leader referred to whenever no one was looking.

The rocky surface welled up in front of them as they walked and the dense trees thinned out as if a path was looming. The leader suddenly threw his hands into the air and shouted 'STOP'.

The cliff appeared suddenly at the edge of the trees and way below, almost out of sight, was the path they were looking for. As far as you could see in either direction were the tops of trees that were so small that they looked like small plants. The map was correct but no one had noticed the dark contour alongside the path that indicated the massive cliff that now blocked their way.

James's picture suddenly became dark and the enthusiasm of moments before disappeared into oblivion. There seemed to be no way to get back to civilization without retracing their tracks and they had been out of telephone communication for the past two days. Their food had almost all been eaten and three of the five Scouts were past the stage of self-motivation and totally dependent on the encouragement of James and his leader.

They all sat quietly as the situation engulfed them and suddenly James could hear his father speak through the wind. He listened intently and all he could hear was "Follow me and work with the energies". James jumped to his feet and said at the top of his voice, "Everyone up, we have to keep moving".

The shock of James's uncharacteristic outburst hit everyone with a thud and their reflexes took over just as they did in emergency training. "Packs on, double pace, we must move." The response was immediate. James called on the energies of the land and the wisdom of the trees, as his grandfather had taught him and the little group immediately felt the energies rise beneath them and deliver a thrust that made their movement effortless. The trees came alive and a feeling of wellbeing engulfed each individual. James was recognized as the new leader and everyone followed as he ran headlong towards the hill that they had avoided an hour earlier.

The path that James selected was steep and rough but it was the quickest way to the top. "Use the trees!" James yelled between breaths, "hook your energy on and throw yourself to the top." The excitement rose and the harmony of movement became a dance as they skillfully encountered obstacle after obstacle and leapt towards the summit.

The distant whir of an engine starting filled James's consciousness and before the sound appeared, he lifted his pace and started to leave the others behind.

He sensed that he had about thirty seconds to clear the trees and somehow signal the helicopter that was about to ready itself for takeoff. His pace increased and he heard his father once more. "Picture the result and leave the detail to someone else."

He burst through the trees and as the sun hit his safety jacket, it lit up the cabin of the helicopter with a flash that shocked the pilot into shutting down the engine immediately. They were safe.

The rescue helicopter was on a routine flight of inspection when the pilot had a strong signal to land the aircraft. He found nothing wrong but he could not get the thought of his partner out of his mind the whole time. Bill had died while rescuing an injured girl in these very mountains. As James approached the open door of the helicopter it was like time had been turned back and his partner had returned. Bill's son was the image of his father and he walked with the same air of confidence as a big smile appeared on his exhausted face.

You will notice the flow of synchronicity and the interwoven assistance of the energies of the earth, each individual and the trees.

The smooth interaction of James's father, Bill, with the wind, the helicopter and his old rescue partner is part of the action of James's personal supercomputer that heads off and takes over the tasks that are needed to produce the simplicity and magic of the ultimate rescue.

Chapter 10

For those who aspire to 'consciously access' their personal supercomputer, there are many simple demonstrations that bring to life the supercomputer interface and start it working in your life.

The concept of active energies and energies that are part of your physical makeup will give you a starting point for many interesting hours of action.

If we start from the physical body and its normal outline we can call on many proven examples of the existence of what is called an energy body that is identical to the physical body that retains the original form even if a limb is removed. People still feel their leg after it has been amputated and it is now possible to detect and measure the energy field of the missing leg.

Extensive studies show that a person can affect an object many meters away from themselves and various forms of measurement have been developed to demonstrate this reality. If we reject our present standards of proof of measurement we will find that the best measuring device in the world is the human body.

If we take one more step and take away analysis and opinion we will reveal an unlimited capability to measure, communicate with, and influence almost everything in our life. When you walk into an establishment and know immediately that there is a dangerous person on the other side of the room, you have achieved everything we assumed above without thought or analysis and without knowing you have sent that person a message to keep clear and stay in their own world.

To bring this into your life in your present situation, without looking for abnormal circumstances, all you have to do is start playing with the energies.

It is possible to decouple the energies of the body and mingle them with your human life force to encourage the influx of universal energies that will kick-start your personal supercomputer and allow you to feel its influence in your life.

This sounds complex, but it only works if you see the simplicity and forget about developing a set of rules to define what must be done to make it work.

Every person is different and each one will see the examples and stories in a way that allows them to experiment with their own capabilities until they achieve what they want in their life.

The energies of the body have a natural form based on the electromagnetic field that controls your form. The healthiest situation is when these energies are flexible and moving in such a way that there is a malleable feeling in every part of the body. A young fit person usually meets this criterion but there is nothing to say that this must be the case. The decoupling of the body's energies works just as well with people of all ages.

Decoupling is achieved by allowing the energies to move outside the limits of the body confines without causing shock to the body and it goes like this:

- Stand loosely in a relaxed position and gently sway in whatever direction or manner feels comfortable until you feel your energy field flopping around like a loose cape. It may take several sessions before the feeling appears.

- Continue the movement until a rhythm and a pattern establishes itself. This also may take several sessions.

- Extend the pattern and experiment with other patterns and combinations of patterns. Do this as many times as you feel necessary.

- Listen to the music associated with the rhythm and experiment with placing musical tunes in various parts of your body as the energies move through, around and away from your body. This is a very healing practice that can start the permanent removal of discomfort or disease.

- Extend your energy patterns to integrate with the trees and feel the interaction as the energies move to and from the trees and in and around your body. Once again, a very healing practice.

- Continue until the energies take on their own path and move in and out of the universe in all sorts of patterns gradually enlivening your body and releasing the fixed attachment of your body's energy field.

- A sense of freedom will enter your being and you will release all limitations allowing the energies of the universe to enter your field and activate your personal supercomputer.

From this point onward, your life will take on a different pattern and you will feel free to communicate with the energies of the trees, to influence the movement of a person from a distance, to communicate with the energies of the earth and to change circumstance through a method that you have no idea of explaining. You will now enter the magic world of your personal supercomputer.

Chapter 11

Catherine laughed as she felt the sen.
her energy spinning. Faster and fasᴜ.
zoomed around her until its hum became
rhythmic and harmonious. Her balance was
perfect and she could feel herself lift as she
took her first stride and started to jog.

For months, she had been making her way to
the local sports field as soon as she could get
mobile each morning driven by a distant
feeling that there was an answer to her long-
term disability that no one seemed to
understand. There was a loose wire
somewhere and she knew it. For a few
moments, every two or three days, she would
operate perfectly and her memory was in tact
but just as quickly as this perfection appeared,
it disappeared leaving her disoriented and
sometimes lost without access to her memory
of where she was or how to do anything. Her
balance was poor and she became exhausted
very quickly.

Catherine had depended on the doctors for
more than four years and now that they
declared that nothing more could be done she
had reverted to listening closely and writing
every day to get directions on what to do next.

She had been given a lot of assistance and somewhere in all of that she had found something more than what science could offer. A familiar voice initially from within started to guide her to do things that she had never heard of before.

Each time she wrote there was a thrill in her body and she could feel activity that continued throughout the day and into the night. Her hand coordination improved quickly and a positive feeling of wellbeing started to show itself around her.

Catherine rose quickly one morning determined to get to the sports field and walk among the trees. Everything felt good and the usual pain in her spine was less than normal. Her trips to the field had become a ritual and she looked forward to the clear communication of instructions that she received at the field. Without hesitation, she dressed, picked up her glasses and walked down the short hall to the front door. Everything went out of focus and her head spun with sudden nausea. She stopped quickly knowing that she could fall at any moment and as a reflex action she took off her glasses.

The world suddenly came back into focus and the spinning nausea stopped immediately. The confusion was like a hanging cloud and it took almost a minute before Catherine realized that her glasses had caused the problem.

Catherine opened the door and looked out. Everything was clear. She held up her glasses and the world went out of focus. For some reason after twenty-five years, Catherine no longer needed glasses. She returned her glasses to her room and with a smile headed off to her beloved sports field to continue her instruction in the art of using a body that was not supposed to work.

It was always Catherine's joke that if someone could invent a Helium jacket it would take the load off her back and allow her to get around without the constant distraction of pain. To her delight, the first exercise she was led through was the development of her energy to such an extent that she could expand it out like a hovercraft and lower it to the ground until she felt all the weight lifted from her spine. All her prayers were answered at once and she was so excited that she forgot to thank whomever it was that helped her.

Her response was worth a million thanks and she never got around to saying anything like she imagined she should say under the circumstances. There was too much ahead and so much activity that her time was fully occupied.

She was shown how to send her energy forward and allow herself to be pulled along. How to maintain her balance by spreading the energy and spinning it like a top and how to cushion her vertebra by expanding each joint and filling it with a special 'pink' energy that felt so nurturing it was the total opposite to pain.

She had been taken out at dusk and led through the paths that were renowned for the presence of snakes and shown how her natural defensive instincts were so powerful that everything cleared her path before she got there. The first sudden rustle of the undergrowth almost frightened her to death but when the calm voice came clearly "stand still and send it love" she knew exactly what to do and when to move forward with safety.

She had been shown how to walk backwards and then close her eyes and still know where she was going. It was like she jumped out of her body and looked from another place to direct herself around the bends in the track.

Now was the big test. She was about to run and all the small exercises were about to come together with a special magic a child emanates when running for the first time. Her jog was steady and precise and she looked like a proud stallion prancing in front of a crowd. There was no pain and no sense of hardship as she settled into a rhythm awaiting the command. It came like a shot of a gun "RUN".

Her eyes lit up as she felt the acceleration and out of nowhere, she was running faster than she had ever run in her whole life. Tears of joy filled her eyes as she slowed to a walk and a sudden rush of emotion stopped her in her tracks. She fell to her knees praying with thanks to the God she knew had totally replenished her life.

Each step along the way is another interface with the divine where your personal supercomputer works behind the scene to make it possible and to deliver everything with simplicity into your life.

The extent to which you allow the interface of your personal supercomputer is up to you but there is no denial of its presence and the elegance of its simplicity.

Chapter 12

If we now return to the child and experience its joy and delight with the presence of 'Tinkerbelle Sparkles' we can feel a familiarity without even remembering our childhood. The sparkles seem to be all around us and without much effort at all we can locate each sparkle and feel the effect of its excitement and brilliance.

It may seem strange that this phenomenon is not part of our normal education or research, but like many other things, it has been denigrated to the world of fiction and simply referred to as something associated with fairy tales.

This phenomenon is one of the most important factors of our existence in the physical plane, and at one time, it was well known as part of everyday life.

Without going into the history of what made it necessary to hide this brilliant secret in front of everyone's eyes, we now encourage everyone to take on what they feel and allow the reality of sparkles to be part of their lives.

With this done it is possible, without further proof, to simply start using the amazing capabilities of our sparkles and experiencing what they provide in our life.

The reality is that each sparkle constitutes our connection to another dimension where the magic of our being resides. Our wellbeing, sense of possibility and special connection to the unknown emanate from these points. The true hologram of our being is indicated in the physical plane when all of our sparkles are activated and the resulting brilliance of our being cannot be ignored by anyone. The childlike sparkle of our being is the greatest investment we could ever make in our life and every step that makes this available must be considered more valuable than gold.

Our personal supercomputer comes into action in the activation and coordination of our sparkles and provides the superhuman effects that allow you to use and spread your magic through the delivery of sparkles to people, events and circumstances that are in need of their own magic.

The activation is simple and many times will start as soon as you focus on 'Tinkerbelle Sparkles'.

Each person has his or her own method but one that often works is, with a sense of mischief, quietly reach out and touch a sparkle when it is not paying attention. You will feel it burst into life and in a matter of moments you will feel the thrilling tingle of all the other sparkles following suit. Your energy levels will quickly rise and a lighthearted smile will become a fixture that you cannot remove. Your presence becomes magnificent and your interest in your surroundings becomes prominent. You have entered the world of magic and miracles.

In practical terms, a bright-eyed sparkly person will hold the most significant positions in the world from waitress all the way through to senior executive. Their capabilities, both practical and technical, seem to exceed expectation and their activities and scholastic abilities come with ease. Their natural brilliance seems to breed more brilliance.

For those who wish to experience this brilliance, it is available, and for those who wish to spread their magic with mischief and elegance, it is also available, but first you must acknowledge the presence of your personal supercomputer and be willing to live with 'Tinkerbelle Sparkles' and the joy of a multidimensional existence.

Made in the USA
San Bernardino, CA
17 November 2018